My Walk with GOD

Mother
Elizabeth H. Travers

PAGE PUBLISHING
Conneaut Lake, PA

First originally published by Page Publishing 2022

ISBN 978-1-6624-6701-1 (pbk)
ISBN 978-1-6624-6702-8 (digital)

Printed in the United States of America

My walk with God started in approximately the year 1977. I was looking out the window of my apartment, and this voice spoke to me, saying, "Buy the house on the corner." I could not imagine what it was, but I was standing there, getting high off weed. In 1970, I went to work in a facility, and while working there, I was introduced to marijuana and became addicted. Then I start smoking wacky weed, angel dust, and the whole nine yards.

I maintained a quality lifestyle. I was financially independent, I always went to church on Sunday, and I took my daughter to church. We always went to church. I did not know God, but I knew of God. I grew up in the church. My father was an elder in the Pentecostal Holiness Church, and my mother was one of the mothers of the church.

All my life, I was raised in a family that loved Jesus. But I did not know Jesus. I've always believed in God, but I was just a churchgoer, as I already stated. But I learned the Bible at an early age. One day, I was looking out the window of my apartment and saw the realtors were renovating the apartment across the street from my apartment into single-family homes. I never ever wanted a house, but this voice spoke to me not once but again and again. I actually decided that I should inquire about the houses, and I did. The voice told me to buy the house on the corner. The side window of my apartment faced the single-family homes across the street from me. I called the realtor and made an appointment to meet with her. She showed me the houses that were finished, but the one on the corner was not for sale. She tried very hard to get me interested in another one of the houses, but I told her no. I specifically wanted the one on the corner. She said that I could take her information and that she would take my information so she could inform me when the one on the corner became available; I could have an option to buy it. Well, about two or three months later, she called me and said that the house on the corner had been sold and it would become available upon completion of renovation if I was still interested. I talked to my husband about it. He was very supportive and happy. He wanted…a home. We were told we could come in and sign a contract so whenever it became available, we would have first choice to purchase it if still interested. That was in the spring of 1977. I never forgot the voice that spoke to me to buy the house on the corner while I was getting high.

God speaks to us. Do we listen, or do we hear Him? We did purchase the house on the corner where I live until this day, year 2021, loving Jesus for loving me so much that "He was wounded for our transgressions, He was bruised for our iniquities; The chastisement of our peace was upon Him, and with His stripes we are healed" (Isaiah 53:5 NKJV). He said, "I have power to lay it down, and I have power to take it again." (John 10:18 NKJV).

> For God so loved the world that he gave his
> only begotten SON that whosoever believeth in
> him should not perish but have everlasting life.
> (John 3:16 NKJV)

After I moved into the house a year later, weird things started happening to me, and my mother's body was afflicted with cancer in 1978. She had never been seriously sick in her lifetime. She was a woman of great faith and believed in God for everything. At the time she was afflicted, I felt like my mother was going to leave me. I did not want her to go, so I asked God not to take her. I told God I would do anything, not realizing I was committing my life to God.

Let's get back to when I moved into the house in 1977. Every year on my birthday, I gave a big birthday party that lasted all night long—all the drugs, all the liquor, beer, and wine, and dancing all night. *But* God had a plan. That was my last party. The next year, I was in the process of getting ready for my birthday party when things started happening about four or five days before the party. I was in my kitchen, getting high, and I felt movement in my kitchen. It was as if someone was there with me. I became afraid—so afraid that I threw the weed in the toilet. I began to get paranoid, and right away, I said, "I am not going to have a party." It stayed on my mind, not to have a party, so I called the party off. Everyone was so disappointed (no freebies). That was around November 1978.

About a month later, a coworker and I were shopping one night during Christmas. I was driving down Branch Avenue in Maryland, getting high, when I had an outer darkness experience. I was driving the car, and suddenly I was in outer darkness. I cannot explain it. I must've driven for maybe a half mile or so. I remember I passed Marlow Heights Shopping Center. When I came back to myself, I was about a half mile from the center. Nothing happened. I was just in pure darkness. And I asked my friend, "What happened?" She said, "Nothing." I told her about the experience I had, and she said I was driving the car and nothing happened." I became frightened and threw the joint out the window. I know I was physically there, but my soul was in darkness for a few minutes. Things were happening to me, and I just didn't understand. Then came my conversion in a snowstorm in March 1979 approximately. My dates maybe a little off but not much.

I woke up that morning in March 1979, and snow was up to my knees. All I could hear was that inner voice in my spirit. I was to go walking in the snow, so I got high before I went walking (the best day of my life). As I was walking, I began crying and sobbing to God. And I did not know what was going on. I said three words as I walked: "*Lord, help me.*" *For two miles, as I walked, crying out to God to help me, I never said anything else.* I looked up, and I was in front of one of the mothers' homes that belong to Bible Way Church. I went up and knocked at her door. She invited me in. She didn't know me, but she knew my daughter. She offered me breakfast. I was still crying, and I accepted the coffee only. We did not have any conversation. After a few minutes, she looked at me and said, "Honey, why don't you stop running?" That was all she said. I did not respond.

As I was leaving her home, I looked out the window, and the voice of the Lord said to me, "Look at that bus trying to plow through the snow." I looked at the exhaust pipes as the snow was falling heavily. It was like a black cloud of smoke pouring into the atmosphere. The voice of the Lord said, "I sent the snow to purify the air so many will live and not die." That was the first time, to my knowledge, I have ever heard the voice of God. I don't know how I knew it was God, but I did. So I continued on my journey about two miles and stopped at my girlfriend's house. I was telling my friends what the Lord said to me, but they did not believe me. They said I was tripping. They were getting high, but I did not indulge. I drank some beer and stayed for an hour or so then started my journey back home.

As I walked back, I was telling everyone on the street that God sent the snow to purify the air so many may live. God is so good. The air we were breathing was so polluted. We were breathing poisonous gases and germs into our bodies. Because so many people were getting sick, God sent the snow to purify the air. That snow was made of huge pure-white flakes. It was so beautiful, so white. There is nothing like the handiwork of God. He is so awesome and loves us so much, and He's always looking out for us all the time. You can't help but love Him. I came home from my journey, and I called my sister and told her all the things that happened that day. My sister said to me, "Didn't you say you were going to get baptized?" And it was like a great awakening hit me. I remember I went upstairs that night, got down on my knees, and told Jesus, "Let me live till Sunday. I will give you my life. I will get baptized in the name of Jesus." And I did just that.

I went to church and gave my life to Jesus. I reverenced God as I would my own father because He is the father that breathed life into me and made me a living soul. I fasted and prayed for six months to overcome the strongholds in my life, and then I was filled with the Holy Spirit. It's a free gift from God. I thank God for a repented heart. That is the right way to God.

When I gave my life to Jesus, I was very serious because I know hell is real, and I don't want to go there. I want to spend eternity with

Jesus after all the things He suffered for our salvation, and His love for us is even more than the human mind can comprehend. Nobody, not anybody, can ever love you like the way Jesus does, and I mean nobody.

After giving Christ my life, I began to pursue Him with all diligence, and then I met *Chris.* She was a neighbor I met on the sidewalk outside my house one day, and it was like God Himself brought us together. We began to pray and fellowship together on a regular basis. He used us mightily in prayer. She has gone home to be with the Lord, but she will always remain in my heart. We cherished the gift God had given us and used it to the glory of God. *To God be the glory.*

My mother was now in the process of taking radiation treatments for a short period of time. It was *amazing* how she never suffered or had any pain during her illness—*none.* God gave us two good years with our mother before she went home. She was so ready to go home. She stayed with my sister. She called me one morning and said there was this lady in her room last night that never said anything to her. She just stood there. The next morning, I went over to my sister's house to try and understand what she was saying. She told me about this lady (she thought it was a lady) standing over her bed with a long white dress. She had no face and wore a turban on her head, and she never said anything. She just stood there, so my mother asked her what she wanted. She never answered her. Then she left the room and stood on the steps in the hall, never doing anything. And then she just left. She was not afraid of her; she just didn't understand who or why she was there. We knew it was spiritual but did not understand. I was a babe in Christ, so I went to ask Mother Wells, one of my mothers in the Lord. She said, "Daughter, your mother had a visitation of an angel." That was all she said. I perceived in my spirit the Lord was getting her ready to take her home.

My mother had a great front porch ministry along with her missionary work. She sang on her front porch every evening with a mighty great anointing. Everybody in the neighborhood loved her. People got saved by her singing. Her homegoing was in 1980 at the age of 90. The church was filled to capacity. She was well-loved by all. My mother was also one of the mothers in her church where she served for seventy years, and she loved her church family so much. She talked about how they had renovated the church and how she would like to see it. That was the only thing she ever talked about: Jesus and her church family.

I took her to her home in Virginia and she stayed for about a week to visit so she could go see the church and see my brother, who lives there. I thought it was something that she might like to do. After she returned to Washington, DC, about two weeks later, her bladder stopped functioning, so my sisters insisted on her going to the hospital. But my mother did not want to go. She knew what was going on, and she was ready to go. She asked me to tell them because she knew that I knew, but they insisted she go. So I went with her and stayed with her day and night to be with her because she did not like being in a hospital.

A week later on a Sunday morning, I went to church. That Sunday morning, the pastor of the church I attend preached a sermon from Isaiah 53. He talked about the suffering servant. I had taken some notes. I felt in my spirit the Lord wanted me to share the notes of the sermon with my mother. I shared the sermon with her; it was a message for her. My sister was at the hospital with my mother. Before that Sunday, I had asked God to let me be there whenever she was ready to pass. I would go home in the evening to take care of my personal hygiene, and then my sister would come after work, making sure she was never left alone. I knew her time with us was short and that she was ready.

The next morning, the nurse came to take her blood. My mother told her, "Would you please leave me alone so I can die?" I asked the nurse not to bother her, and she agreed. Then the doctors came later, making their rounds. They spoke with me concerning her condition. My mother never complained, never took any medicine, and did not have any pain, just the peace of God all over her.

My niece came from *Cape Cod* to visit with her. When she walked in, she said, "Auntie, go home and get some rest." I could not leave. I knew it was time. I told her, "Let us make a circle around her and pray." We held hands with her, making a circle around her. As I began to pray, the Holy Spirit said this to me, and I said what he said: "I commend my mother's spirit unto thee." I will never forget that day as long as I live. The room began to fill up with the *glory* of God. Instantly, *angels* were all over the room. It was like a maze or like clouds filled the room up. You could sense it, feel it, but you couldn't see. It was the most beautiful experience I've ever witnessed. When I spoke those words over her, her hands dropped, and the angels took over. What a mighty *God* we serve. He's an *awesome God.* He's an off-the-hook *god*—the Creator of the whole universe. The only reason you don't love Him is because you don't know Him. Falling in love with Jesus is the best thing that has ever happened to me. I thank God that my mother lived to see me get saved. I thank Him for saving me, and I am so glad I am saved. I bless His name, and I will let nothing separate me from His love. I thank God for teaching me how to let go and let God, but I still have Jesus, my first love, sharing my walk.

I was in church service one Tuesday night (my regular fellowship service) when one of the mothers of the church asked me, because I had a car, if I could take a young lady and her two children home. Of course, I said yes. I took them to her boyfriend's apartment where she stayed with the father of one of her children. I volunteered to pick her up for church service because it was a very long way to church from where she lived. I did not know anything about her at the time, and she never call me to pick her up. But she came to church, and I would take her back home.

I developed a good friendship with her as time went on. She never told me anything about herself, but I just continued to be nice to her. Then one night, about 10:00 or 11:00 p.m., she called me and ask me if I could come and get her and her children. She said her boyfriend had put her out. I knew I was going to get her, but I didn't know what my husband was going to say about bringing her home with me; she was a stranger. She was at the trailway bus station waiting, so I prayed and asked the Lord to touch my husband's heart to let her spend the night. And he did. Well, one night when I was ready for church, she said she was not going. I asked her why, and she said her boyfriend was coming to pick her up. I was upset that she didn't say anything to me about it, but I waited for him to pick her up.

She left, but she still came to church. I got to know a little about her and the boyfriend. When I first met her, the baby was about six months old. As time went on, I found out they were homeless. I continued to try and help her and the children. One day, she came by to see me with the children. She did not have a place to go and nowhere to stay. I offered my home to her, and she stayed for a long time. Then we had a misunderstanding one night; she became angry with me and said she was leaving. I asked her to wait till morning and not leave at night. She made a phone call and left. She dropped a slip of paper in the trash can when she left. I got it and read the phone number; it was to child protective services. I called them and told them what happened out of concern for her and her children and of where she was going that time of night.

The counselor gave me a little insight into her situation. She was homeless, and her children were in and out of foster homes. The older boy was about eight years old, and the baby was about six months old. The counselor asked me if he could take my information because they didn't know anyone who knew her. I gave him my information and told him I did not know her either and that I had met her at my church. Well, about five months later, my phone rang one day, and the lady on the phone said, "I am a lawyer representing two young boys, and we don't know anything about them or their mother. We would like for you to come to court. We are going to take her children into custody. We would like for someone to be there that knows them." Of course, I insisted that I didn't know her either and that I had just met her in church and tried to help but was not successful. Well, they subpoenaed her to court, and she didn't show up. So I left.

The next day, as I walked into the house from work, the phone was ringing. It was the children's lawyer. She said to me, "We put out a writ for her. We will lock her up overnight, and the children will be placed in foster care." Then she asked me if I would come to court again the next day. I said, "No, I have to go to work. I was already there one day."

The next day, when I came in from work, the phone was ringing again, and it was the children's lawyer. She told me what happened in court and asked me if I would take her children into foster care. I thought that she was tripping me. A foster mother? Never ever. Then she said that when the *judge* ordered her children to be put into foster care, the young lady ask the *judge* to let me foster them. I don't know what was going on in that courtroom and how I got into this, but it was absolutely unbelievable. And the *judge* consented. I told her she would have to give me time to pray about this. Well, God was in the plan. I did take the children after praying about it. I was not too happy about it, but after I thought about it, I said to myself, "Here is a woman that doesn't know me, and *a judge* that does not know me either granted her this request. It must be God."

I did not only have her children; I also was there for her at all times. I grew to love her as if she were my very own. Morning, noon, or night, I was always there for her whenever she called. She ended up having six children, and I kept in touch with all of them so that they would not grow up without knowing their brothers and sister and their mother. After six years in foster care, my husband and I adopted the two boys. All six of her children but one got to know her because he died. He was one month old. The rest got to know each other, and she was united with her family and her brothers and sisters also before she went home to be with the Lord. I loved her, but most of all, God loved her and brought her into my life. And I cannot take the credit. But I thank God for using me. All the glory goes to God, for we are nothing without Him and can't do anything without Him. This relationship with her lasted twenty-seven years. The remaining three children are still in God's care and are doing very well, and I try to keep up with them.

While at my present job, I had a mind to change jobs. It just stayed on my mind, so I began looking for a job elsewhere. I filled out applications for several places, and one place came to my mind. That was not one of my choices, so I dismissed that one from my list. But it kept coming to me, so I decided to apply for a job there. I filled out the application, and the personal manager, who took the forms, informed me that they were not hiring but that they would contact me when something became available. I saw her put my forms at the bottom of the other applications, and I watched her do it. Well, in about a month, she called me and asked me if I would come in for an interview, and I said yes. I went in for an interview and was hired.

After being employed there, another significant event happened. There was a canteen where employees ate lunch. I went there on my lunch break each day for about a month. I did not know anyone there. As I was walking back, this young lady walked up to me and politely asked me if I was a Christian. I said yes. She then responded, "I wonder if you and I could meet for lunch and pray sometimes." I said yes, but I told her I was a new employee and that she would have to make her lunch time compatible with mine.

We started to have lunch frequently and came to be the best of friends. We started praying and studying the Bible on our phones at home. At work, we started going to the prayer chapel at lunch time to pray and meditate on the Word. Other Christians heard about us and began to come to the prayer chapel. The Lord really began to bless the young lady that came to me and started this on-the-job lunch hour prayer.

One day, she gave me her testimony. She said she asked God to send someone to help her and that I was the person that God sent to her. The Lord restored her and brought her back to him in that prayer chapel. The Lord did some great work in that prayer chapel where other Christians were healed, delivered, set free, strengthened, and gave their lives back to Christ. We had some great meetings in that prayer chapel. When you think of the faithfulness in God our Father, it is more than our human mind can understand. Thank the Lord for the Holy Spirit that lives in the born-again believers. We were praying for the patients and the whole facility.

The Lord moved in a very special way. One morning, we were in the report room, changing shifts, when Code Blue came over the speaker. That meant every available person must go immediately to the unit. We were running to the patient's room, and I began to slow down. They were giving the patient CPR. The ambulance was called to the floor to take him to another hospital. As I was leaving the room, the Holy Spirit said, "Go pray." I said, "I am on duty. How can I?" Then He showed me the bathroom. I went straight to the bathroom, and the Holy Spirit began to make intercession for the soul of that man while I was weeping and crying. When I came out of the bathroom a little later on, the driver came back to the unit and told us he had expired. The Holy Spirit said that his soul was saved.

What a mighty God we serve. He is so true to His word because He is the Word, and the Word is God. He let me find favor with my supervisor, who was head RN on my unit. One day, she called me to her office and told me to be careful. She knew I was a Christian, and she was too. But they were watching me. She was so nice to me. She knew I was praying for the patients. It was not allowed by the staff, but God has a way that no man understands. "And we know that all things work together for the good to those that love God—to they who are called according to His purpose" (Romans 8:28 NKJV).

Another morning, one of our patients was getting ready to leave us. God is amazing. We knew he was getting ready to expire. I walked into his room. No one was there, but when I was in the room, he told me to shut that light off. "It is so bright I can't see." He repeated it over again: "Cut the light out. It is too bright." I knew he was talking about the light—Jesus. That afternoon, he went home to be with the Lord, so peaceful and so quiet.

Well, the Holy Spirit had been ministering to me, telling me to resign, and I was undecided because I did not think I was supposed to resign; I was too young. I was not thinking about the two boys I had to raise. Well, one day in the prayer chapel, one of the saints said, "Mother, you are going to be leaving us. The Lord said the enemy is after you." I received it because the Holy Spirit had been speaking to me about it, and that confirmed what he had said: for me to resign. About two months later, I resigned.

I'd like to share part of my walk in 1988. The enemy attacked me with breast cancer (but God). I had a mammogram, and it showed a spot on my left breast. The doctor did a biopsy and said it was malignant, and they wanted to do surgery. I called my pastor, Bishop Williams, and a mother at my church; and after prayer, I consented to have the surgery. I was a babe in Christ, and when I went that morning to have the surgery, I had been prepped and was on the stretcher, on my way to the operating room, when I heard the Holy Spirit say to me, "I am the Lord thy God that healeth thee." I knew he was going to heal me. I didn't know what to do, so I had the surgery. My left breast was removed, but (God) after the surgery, the doctor said he was disappointed when they went in; they did not find any cancer. I was totally healed. After that, they scanned my whole body, looking for cancer, but there was none. Everybody said, "Why don't you sue them?" I said, "No, it is not always about money. I am just thankful that the Lord healed me, and I never had to have any radiation or anything." Thank the Lord.

Back in the 1980s, my church used to fellowship on Sunday with other churches having evening services. A group of us would go and support our ministers on a Sunday night. A group of us was at this church one day. Back then, the word of knowledge would go forth, and the ministers would prophesy to the people. At a church one Sunday night, toward the end of the service, the minister said, "Someone in the service tonight, death is coming to your house. If that person will come forth, I will pray for them." Of course, we were all looking around at one another, not knowing who it was, so nobody went forth. When the elder was leaving the church, we asked him what would happen if that person did not come forth. Elder Duckett said, "I will be praying for that person and their home." I did not even think that it was me.

Well, about three days later on a Wednesday night, about 10:00 p.m., I was reading and meditating on the Word of God. I was at my kitchen table, and I could not go to sleep. This weird feeling came over me. It is so hard to explain that horrible feeling. I kept reading, and it got so intense that I stopped and started praying. It was like a sticky, icky, cold, moisture feeling, and it was all over the room. And then I remembered what the elder had said that Sunday night. I began to pray and pray, then I had a vision of the death angel. He was upstairs in my bedroom, hovering over my husband. He was asleep. I prayed and prayed and prayed for what felt like a very long, long time. I kept praying until I felt the release, and then he went away. My husband was sleeping, so he did not know what had happened. The Holy Spirit told me not to tell him until the appointed time, so

I waited for the Holy Spirit's time before I told him. We know that all things work together for good to they that love GOD—to they who are the called according to His purpose. At the appointed time, I told him, and it was a real blessing; that was in the 1980s. My husband did not go home to be with the Lord until the year of 2016. Hallelujah.

Another part of my walk I'd like to share involved my brother. My brother had been sick a long time, and the doctor was going to place him in a nursing home. I was standing outside his hospital room, crying, and the Lord told me to take him home with me. I fasted for forty days for him, and an interesting thing happened at the end of the fortieth day. It just so happened to be Christmas day that morning. While I was in the kitchen, cooking, I heard these big black birds. They flew over my house by the hundreds and landed on the trees all around my neighborhood. They stayed in the trees, chattering for a long period of time, and then they all flew away. I am not saying it had anything to do with my fast, but it was so weird that it happened that morning. As it turned out, God added two years to my brother's life, and he enjoyed the rest of his life before he went home to be with the Lord.

I had four brothers and three sisters. One day, one of my sisters was getting ready to go home to be with the Lord, and I felt in my spirit it was not her time. So I asked the Lord why she was leaving us. He said she didn't want to stay here and that He would not take her will from her because she wanted to leave here, so He took her home. That was a lesson for me. God will not take your will from you. You must submit your will to God.

God is so awesome. I had a stroke in 2019, and I never had any physical or mental aftereffects from it whatsoever. At that time, I did not know I was having a stroke, and I was out and about in my daily routine. I knew something was wrong, but I could not tell what was going on. I called my grandson, who is my pastor, Yusef, to pray for me. After I went to physical therapy, I made another run. Shortly after, I went to a shopping center. Eventually, I called my daughter and told her I needed to go to the ER. Upon arriving there, they rushed me to get a CAT scan. I was then informed that I was having or had a stroke but that there were still no symptoms, so I stayed overnight for observation. I signed myself out the next morning then went home. I called my PCP to inform her what was going on, and she said I should not have left the hospital. I told her the treatment there was awful, but she informed me to go to another hospital. And I did. They kept saying the same thing to me: all x-rays showed I had a stroke, but everything in my body was functioning normally. They kept me under observation for twenty-four hours, and I was released afterward. I've since never had another problem with that. Thank God. That was in 2019, and this is 2021. He is still healing and delivering. Thank You, Jesus. God is awesome.

When God filled me with His spirit in 1979, I was at home with my daughter, Carol, and my grandson, Yusef. I manifested for about an hour in the spirit. I kept picking up my grandson again and again and again. He is now my pastor. God is awesome. He prepared him at the age of four. After I moved into the house, He saved me and told me, "I put you on that corner for My purpose."

A few years later, when my grandchild Pete was about was nine years old and my other grandchild Yusef was four years old, I started a group of children every Saturday in my home with a prayer and Bible study. I named them Young Children for Jesus. They learned Bible verses and how to pray. They really enjoyed being there, and we developed a relationship with one another and their families. After that, we would go out and have some type of recreation and light food. I took them to church, and most of them got baptized. One young man prayed so hard for his mother to get saved, and God did just that. He saved her. When they became teenagers, they sort of drifted apart, but the seeds were already planted. We kept in touch with one another. Most of them are still in church today as evangelists, or deacons, and I still keep in touch with a few of them to this day, thirty-five years later.

One young man I helped his mother and took care of him until she was able. I am still in touch with them. It has been over thirty years ago since then, and we still have love in our hearts for one another. And there was this young lady who had five children and was in a hard situation. I helped her. She and her family are still with

Jesus, and Jesus has really blessed them to be prosperous. There are many others like the two. To God be the glory. That is why we are here. He saved us to be our brother's keeper and to love our neighbors as ourselves.

On the side of my house, there is a huge sign with the name Jesus on it that has been such a blessing to this entire community and those that do not live in this community. It was about 1985 when I had in mind the idea to make a sign with just the name Jesus. It was around Christmas. I took wire clothes hangers, shaped the letters in to his name, Jesus, and wrapped Christmas lights around the wires so the name would light up. It was so beautiful, and everyone would tell me about it. People would come in their cars and sit and look at the name Jesus. After Christmas that year, I decided to keep it because it was such a blessing to everyone, and I still have the Jesus sign lit up every night until now, 2021. But because of the maintenance with the lights, as my husband and I got older, I had to change the sign. It is now a huge wooden sign with green letters and a spotlight on it, saying "Jesus." People come from all over the city to see the Christmas celebration at Christmastime, representing the true meaning of Christmas and the birth of our Lord and Savior, Jesus. Christmas in my yard display. We just got to lift up the name of Jesus.

One neighbor told me, "When I get to your house in the morning on my way to work, it is dark outside, but when I see the name Jesus, I know I can make it."

A young lady high on drugs told me, "Don't ever take it down."

When I would take it down to change the lights, everyone would say, "Where is the sign?"

One of my neighbor's sons was high on PCP. He stripped his clothes off and was naked outside. He broke a section of my fence and came into my yard, and he said he was trying to get to Jesus, whose name was on the sign on the side of the house. There is power in the name of Jesus.

One of my sisters in the Lord worked at the Pentagon. She told me one of her coworkers was telling her one day about the house in the neighborhood with the big Jesus sign on it, not knowing that she knew me. The sign has been such a blessing to so many people. The Lord said, "If I be lifted up from the earth I will draw all men unto me."

When God saved me, He call me to a life of prayer. I was placed on that corner for a reason. I know that it was in the plan of God. I pray and hope to God that I will accomplish whatever I am here for to bring glory to God and so that He can get the glory, not me. To God be the glory for the things He has done. He will not share His glory. *He* is the creator of the whole universe, the beginning and the end, the first and the last, and the alpha and omega. He created everything on the earth, everything under the earth, and everything above the earth. Everything belongs to God.

> The earth is the LORD's and the fullness thereof the world and they that dwell therein.
> (Psalms 24:1 KJV)

In our fellowship at the hospital, one of the sisters prayed for the Lord to send her help, one of the ladies there was also a Christian, and the enemy attacked her mind and tried to take her mind. But the Lord is so faithful. For about six months, we stayed in constant warfare, battling the enemy; but God bought her through. He totally delivered and set her free. A few years later, she was called to be a pastor; she is now the pastor of the Lord's church. God can do anything but fail.

I was in the prison ministry at my first church before I went to join my grandson. That prison ministry was the most rewarding ministry. I really enjoyed the fellowship with the men and women. I remember one Sunday morning, when I was on my way to Lorton, the devil tried to kill me. If I did not have the Word in my heart to speak it over my life, I would not have made it. Hallelujah, to God be the glory.

When my grandson was called to be a pastor, I left my first church to go and support him. My former pastor gave me his blessings, saying that was the right thing to do, and he blessed my grandson too. He started in a hotel conference room in Waldorf, Maryland. The year was 2014. My former pastor, the late *Bishop James Silver*, where I was a member for twenty-five years—*Bible Way Temple* on New Jersey Avenue, Washington, DC, opened the church doors for my grandson to have his first- and second-year anniversary services there. To God be the glory. That is the love of Jesus. There are no separate churches. *Jesus is the head of all churches.*

I am a community leader that works very hard for my community and has good relationships with my neighbors. On Christmas every year, I have a twelve-piece nativity scene about 4 ft. tall in my yard. People come every year to admire the true meaning of Christmas, and I try to remind everyone about Jesus. When my grandson opened his church in the year 2014, I hosted a 5:00 a.m. prayer line for others to join me in prayer not just for our church but for the whole body of Christ and all the nations of the world. I have been praying in the mornings for over forty years ever since the Lord saved me. We are at a critical time in America. Ever since the Lord saved me I have kept thanking Him for the mind to go forth in prayer. The Lord tells us to go forth in prayer. Our communication with our real Father, who gave us the breath of life, is prayer.

He is an awesome god we serve. He has blessed me to live to see four generations, and they all are saved. My first great-great-grandchild, Bella Rae, was born in April 2021.

Proverbs 22:6 said, "Train up a child in the way he should go and when he is old, he will not depart from it," so when my grandchildren were young, I always talked to them about Jesus. I told you about my ministry with the children in my community. I always remember how I was raised, and after God saved me, I remember the Word of God. And as they grew in life, the seed that was planted also grew. God saved my daughter, and she took them to church. (He saved my whole family.) Then came my great-grandchildren. They spent every other weekend with me so my family would grow up together and know one another. I taught them about Jesus, and we spent good quality time together. Also, four other young boys— Kelvin, Alijah, Terrance, and Ashton—will always be in my heart. We went everywhere together during summer vacations; we travelled to beaches, amusement parks, and up and down the East Coast. Their favorite spots were Virginia Beach and Great Wolf Lodge. God is so amazing He gave me the mothers too. A life serving God is an amazing life. What He does for one He will do for all because He loves all of us the same, and Jesus died for the sins of the whole world.

Years ago, someone spoke into my life, "I would be the mother of many children," and it came to pass. To God be the glory.

> Who hath saved us, and called us with an holy calling, not according to our works, but according to His own purpose and grace, which was given us in Christ Jesus before the world began. (2 Timothy 1:9)

I was and still am married to the most wonderful man in the world although he is at home with Jesus. I could not have had a better husband handpicked by my mother. To God be the glory for the things he has done. He always encouraged me and supported me in the Lord's work. I am a mother to so many people in my community; some call me Ma, some call me Grandma, some say Ms. Liz, and some say Mrs. Travers and granny. But most of all, I thank God for the respect from them up and down my street throughout my community. They come to me for all types of problems, spiritual and natural. I thank the Lord for that.

There was a young lady who used to prostitute on the corner near my house. She would always say, "Pray for me" (true story). God saved her. She has a government job. Working every day gave her children back to her and moved her in a nice apartment across the street in the same neighborhood. She also has a nice SUV. Look at what the Lord can do. She is a living witness of what the Lord can do—a witness for everyone and for the young ladies that are still out there. Thank You, Jesus.

I have been a community activist for years, serving my community in different capacities and lifting up Jesus in the process. I was a 6CO1 advisory neighborhood commissioner, 7F ANC, and in the 6 district police citizens advisory council since 1977. I was part of the Orange Hats patrol in 6C01. I conducted a prayer and Bible Study in my home and volunteered in the DC jail ministry, in nursing homes, and in church services. And in every service, I'd be *lifting* up the name of Jesus. I also had my street ministry on Minnesota Ave. in the 1980s; on the parking lot, I passed out gospel literature and magazines and prayed for those who needed Jesus. I am currently hosting the prayer line for the Lord's church every morning at 5:00 a.m. and on Saturdays at 7:00 a.m.

Sunday is the Lord's day. We go to His house to worship Him in spirit and in truth, and we also go there to praise Him and assemble ourselves to give Him glory. He loves for His people to come together to fellowship and to honor Him for just being God. It is all about Jesus's death, burial, and resurrection.

The Lord has blessed me with another little girl in 2019. When her mother told me she was pregnant, the Holy Spirit said, "She is an answer to a prayer." I knew then I was going to be in her little life for some reason that only God knows, and I have fallen in love with her as if she were my own. I spoke Jesus into her spirit. God has a way that no man can understand. Dioni's future is in His hands, and so is yours. Give your life to Him because He loves you; it's just as simple as that. And you need to trust Him.

I thank God for my daughter that lives with me, Carol. I really appreciate her love for me and also her trying to be my mother in my aging years. She loves me so much. *Thank you, Carol.* God, bless my son Brandon. The Lord loves him, and he loves the Lord. Pray for him that he will turn his life back over to Jesus. Lord, bless my daughter *Maria.* Keep her in your prayers and her family too. We all need prayer. Thank God for the house on the corner where I have lived for forty-four years, lifting up the name of Jesus, and for such a great life in Him. Jesus, I will never forget what you have done for me and are still doing. *I thank* God for my eighty-eight years. As I write this for the glory of God, my hope is that someone will be inspired to accept Jesus as their Lord and Savior and to know that He loved them so much that He hung on a cross just for them. I am healthy mentally, physically, and most of all, spiritually. I invite you to try Jesus. As a matter of fact, I challenge you to do so. Even if you think you've tried everything else, try Jesus. I would like to extend an invitation to you. Please do not leave this world without saying this from your heart. Ask God to forgive you for your sins in the name of Jesus. Say this: "That if thou confess with thy mouth the Lord Jesus, and shall believe in thine heart that God hath rasied him from the dead, thou shall be saved. For with the heart man believeth unto righteousness; and with the mouth confession is made unto salvation" (Romans 10:9–10).

> Behold I stand at the door and knock: if any man hear my voice, and open the door, I will come in to him and will dine with him, and he with me. (Revelation 3:20)

One of my favorite scriptures is Psalms 51:1–17:

> 1 Have mercy upon me, O God, according to thy lovingkindness: according unto the multitude of thy tender mercies blot out my transgressions. 2 Wash me throughly from mine iniquity, and cleanse me from my sin. 3 For I acknowledge my transgressions: and my sin is ever before me. 4 Against thee, thee only, have I sinned, and done this evil in thy sight: that thou mightest be justified when thou speakest, and be clear when thou judgest. 5 Behold, I was shapen in iniquity; and in sin did my mother conceive me. 6 Behold, thou desirest truth in the inward parts: and in the hidden part thou shalt make me to know wisdom. 7 Purge me with hyssop, and I shall be clean: wash me, and I shall be whiter than snow. 8 Make me to hear joy and gladness; that the bones which thou hast broken may rejoice. 9 Hide thy face from my sins, and blot out all mine iniquities. 10 Create in me a clean heart, O God; and renew a right spirit within me. 11 Cast me not away from thy presence; and take not thy holy spirit from me. 12 Restore unto me the joy of

thy salvation; and uphold me with thy free spirit. 13 Then will I teach transgressors thy ways; and sinners shall be converted unto thee. 14 Deliver me from bloodguiltiness, O God, thou God of my salvation: and my tongue shall sing aloud of thy righteousness. 15 O Lord, open thou my lips; and my mouth shall shew forth thy praise. 16 For thou desirest not sacrifice; else would I give it: thou delightest not in burnt offering. 17 The sacrifices of God are a broken spirit: a broken and a contrite heart, O God, thou wilt not despise.

It will open up your heart to God and let you speak to Him about some of the things you need to say to Him. He is your heavenly Father that loves you more than you love yourself. I will be sharing some scriptures in the Word of God that will be a blessing to you.

1 There was a man of the Pharisees, named Nicodemus, a ruler of the Jews: 2 The same came to Jesus by night, and said unto him, Rabbi, we know that thou art a teacher come from God: for no man can do these miracles that thou doest, except God be with him. 3 Jesus answered and said unto him, Verily, verily, I say unto thee, Except a man be born again, he cannot see the kingdom of God. 4 Nicodemus saith unto him, How can a man be born when he is old? can he enter the second time into his mother's womb, and be born? 5 Jesus answered, Verily, verily, I say unto thee, Except a man be born of water and of the Spirit, he cannot enter into the kingdom of God. 6 That which is born of the flesh is flesh; and that which is born of the Spirit is spirit. 7 Marvel not that I said unto thee, Ye must be born again. 8 The wind bloweth where it listeth, and thou hearest the sound thereof, but canst not

tell whence it cometh, and whither it goeth: so is every one that is born of the Spirit. 9 Nicodemus answered and said unto him, How can these things be? 10 Jesus answered and said unto him, Art thou a master of Israel, and knowest not these things? 11 Verily, verily, I say unto thee, We speak that we do know, and testify that we have seen; and ye receive not our witness. 12 If I have told you earthly things, and ye believe not, how shall ye believe, if I tell you of heavenly things? 13 And no man hath ascended up to heaven, but he that came down from heaven, even the Son of man which is in heaven. 14 And as Moses lifted up the serpent in the wilderness, even so must the Son of man be lifted up: 15 That whosoever believeth in him should not perish, but have eternal life. 16 For God so loved the world, that he gave his only begotten Son, that whosoever believeth in him should not perish, but have everlasting life. 17 For God sent not his Son into the world to condemn the world; but that the world through him might be saved. 18 He that believeth on him is not condemned: but he that believeth not is condemned already, because he hath not believed in the name of the only begotten Son of God. 19 And this is the condemnation, that light is come into the world, and men loved darkness rather than light, because their deeds were evil. 20 For every one that doeth evil hateth the light, neither cometh to the light, lest his deeds should be reproved. 21 But he that doeth truth cometh to the light, that his deeds may be made manifest, that they are wrought in God. (John 3:1–21)

1 And when the day of Pentecost was fully come, they were all with one accord in one place.

2 And suddenly there came a sound from heaven as of a rushing mighty wind, and it filled all the house where they were sitting. 3 And there appeared unto them cloven tongues like as of fire, and it sat upon each of them. 4 And they were all filled with the Holy Ghost, and began to speak with other tongues, as the Spirit gave them utterance. 5 And there were dwelling at Jerusalem Jews, devout men, out of every nation under heaven. 6 Now when this was noised abroad, the multitude came together, and were confounded, because that every man heard them speak in his own language. 7 And they were all amazed and marvelled, saying one to another, Behold, are not all these which speak Galilaeans? 8 And how hear we every man in our own tongue, wherein we were born? 9 Parthians, and Medes, and Elamites, and the dwellers in Mesopotamia, and in Judaea, and Cappadocia, in Pontus, and Asia, 10 Phrygia, and Pamphylia, in Egypt, and in the parts of Libya about Cyrene, and strangers of Rome, Jews and proselytes, 11 Cretes and Arabians, we do hear them speak in our tongues the wonderful works of God. 12 And they were all amazed, and were in doubt, saying one to another, What meaneth this? 13 Others mocking said, These men are full of new wine. 14 But Peter, standing up with the eleven, lifted up his voice, and said unto them, Ye men of Judaea, and all ye that dwell at Jerusalem, be this known unto you, and hearken to my words: 15 For these are not drunken, as ye suppose, seeing it is but the third hour of the day. 16 But this is that which was spoken by the prophet Joel; 17 And it shall come to pass in the last days, saith God, I will pour out of my Spirit upon all flesh: and your

sons and your daughters shall prophesy, and your young men shall see visions, and your old men shall dream dreams: 18 And on my servants and on my handmaidens I will pour out in those days of my Spirit; and they shall prophesy: 19 And I will shew wonders in heaven above, and signs in the earth beneath; blood, and fire, and vapour of smoke: 20 The sun shall be turned into darkness, and the moon into blood, before the great and notable day of the Lord come: 21 And it shall come to pass, that whosoever shall call on the name of the Lord shall be saved. (Acts 2:1–21)

37 Now when they heard this, they were pricked in their heart, and said unto Peter and to the rest of the apostles, Men and brethren, what shall we do? 38 Then Peter said unto them, Repent, and be baptized every one of you in the name of Jesus Christ for the remission of sins, and ye shall receive the gift of the Holy Ghost. 39 For the promise is unto you, and to your children, and to all that are afar off, even as many as the Lord our God shall call. 40 And with many other words did he testify and exhort, saying, Save yourselves from this untoward generation. 41 Then they that gladly received his word were baptized: and the same day there were added unto them about three thousand souls. (Acts 2:37–41)

5 This then is the message which we have heard of him, and declare unto you, that God is light, and in him is no darkness at all. 6 If we say that we have fellowship with him, and walk in darkness, we lie, and do not the truth: 7 But if we walk in the light, as he is in the light, we have fellowship one with another, and the blood of Jesus

Christ his Son cleanseth us from all sin. 8 If we say that we have no sin, we deceive ourselves, and the truth is not in us. 9 If we confess our sins, he is faithful and just to forgive us our sins, and to cleanse us from all unrighteousness. 10 If we say that we have not sinned, we make him a liar, and his word is not in us. (1 John 1:5–10)

The Bible is the awesome Word of God. It is in Him that we live and breathe hallelujah. Try Jesus. It is all about Jesus—His death, burial, and resurrection. Give Him the glory. The Holy Spirit inspired me to write this and name it *My Walk with God*.

WORKS CITED

The Holy Bible: King James Version. KAPPA Books Publishers, LLC, 2019.

The Holy Bible: NKJV, New King James Version. Thomas Nelson Publishers, 2011.

About the Author

It was about two years ago when the Holy Spirit spoke to Elizabeth to write this book and title it *My Walk with God*. This is her personal testimony about her life in Christ. She was reluctant to do so because of her age. At the time, she was eighty-seven years old in the year of 2019. Another blessing would be bestowed upon Elizabeth that same year. The Holy Spirit ministered to her to go on an ocean cruise with Bishop T. D. Jakes. She had no mind to go on the cruise, but as she listened to the Holy Spirit, everyday it kept coming to her to go on the cruise, and then He specified to go alone. She did not understand why she was to go alone, so eventually she called and registered to go on the cruise. The lady said to her, "You know, there are women who would like to share rooms and would you be interested in sharing?" At the time, Elizabeth remembered that she was supposed to go alone, but she felt in her spirit with someone she did not know. Of course, she picked the room that she wanted and accepted the roommate, which was a wonderful pastor from Los Angeles, and everything worked out fine.

"The Holy Spirit knows how to do all things because He knows all things." They are still corresponding with each other. Two years later, Elizabeth had a revelation of why she went alone but will not share. Truly, it was a great, great blessing. By the way, there were predominantly all Christians on the boat. She found it so inspiring and absolutely fantastic. She met so many beautiful people who love the Lord in the body of Christ and still correspond with them. By the inspiration of the Holy Spirit, Elizabeth is attempting to write this book for God's glory. Her prayer is that it will be a blessing to whomever should read it, especially the unsaved population and, of course, her brothers and sisters in the Lord. "We can do all things through Christ. For without Jesus, we are nothing and can do nothing without Him. I feel like time is winding up for everybody, so let all of us be about winning souls for Jesus. That is why He saved us. To go into the streets and the byways and tell them about Jesus and His love for them." At the end of the book, you will know why. Elizabeth is now eighty-eight years old and accepted Jesus Christ as her Savior in the year 1978—the blessed year of her life. She was about to self-destruct (but God, but God). She was raised in the church, and all her life, she went to church; but later in life, she became addicted to drugs. She never accepted Jesus in her heart as her Savior until the blessed day of her life, March 1978. That was her conversion in the snow, which you have read earlier on. "There is no other way for eternal life, but through Jesus Christ, who loves us so much and gave His life for us." In three months, November 2021, Elizabeth will be eighty-nine years of age. All her spiritual life she has taught her children, grandchildren, great-grandchildren, and now her great great-granddaughter. All her family are now saved. It has not been easy; Elizabeth's family has been through a lot, dealing with all type of crisis (but God, but God). "Love conquers evil. Jesus' love is the greatest of all love and there is no other love like His. You have never been loved until you have experienced the love of Jesus."

Many years ago, Elizabeth was on her way to church, and one Sunday, there was a young man standing outside Bible Way Temple asking for money. She gave him God's blessing and kept walking. He would be out there every Sunday asking for money, and she would keep walking. This went on for three or four Sundays. Then one Sunday, she stopped and asked him to go to church with her; he was "homeless, dirty, smelly, and looking rough." He replied, "Will you take me to church looking like this?" and Elizabeth said, "Yes." He said, "If you take me looking like this, then I'll go." He went with her and sat right beside her in church. She gave him money to put in the offering, and after church, they went to his favorite Carryout for lunch and then she took him to the shelter. Every Sunday, he would be outside when she would go to church, and he would go to church with her. This went on for two or three months, and they went to church together. He was still "smelly and dirty." Elizabeth would always feed him, give him a couple of dollars, and take him to the shelter. She gave him her home number so he could contact her. This went on for three or four months afterward. They talked on the phone sometimes. She always encouraged him, and he liked to joke with her. She enjoyed their conversations, and he would always say to her, "I am pimping you, pretty lady." That was what he always called her. Elizabeth went on in the church and sat in the balcony as she normally would. People would look at him funny because he was so "dirty," but they kept right on going to church together. One Sunday, he was not outside when she went to church. She went on to church and took her seat in the balcony at Bible Way Temple, the service was in progress, and she happened to look around and thought she saw him, so she looked back again. Elizabeth could not believe her eyes. There he was, sitting two rows behind her. She got up and told him to come sit with her. He was dressed up with a suit, shirt, tie, shaved, haircut, and looking like a king. She was so happy. He wanted to surprise her. That was the beginning of a very long friendship. Elizabeth's husband also liked him and talked to him on the phone to encourage him.

Long story short, one day, he called Elizabeth and told her he was living with his daughter, and he had got counseling and assistance from the D.C. government. He became a responsible citizen. All because of the love that Jesus had for him and just used her as an instrument. "It is always about Jesus and His love for mankind. Thank You, Jesus, for Your agape love. We search all our lives looking for peace and love, but we will never find it in drugs, alcohol, sex, money, or success. True love only comes from Jesus." Elizabeth prays and hope someone will be inspired to accept Jesus as their Savior and believe that God raised Him from the dead. He hung on the cross and gave His life just for us. He is a real and a true living God. His spirit lives inside of me. The Holy Spirit, which we all need. This is her story to the best of her ability with the help of the Holy Spirit, praying that many lives will be touched and inspired to seek the Lord Jesus Christ.

Intercessory prayer warrior and missionary called by God, appointed by Jesus and anointed by the Holy Spirit.

1973

2019

Elizabeth and Husband

Jesus sign on my house